Political Criticisms & Treatise On Socio-Capitalism

By: Thomas Glenn

I've written this series of political criticisms and treatise on a socio-capitalistic platform not for political gain or to encourage dissent but to promote rationally and intellectually moral thought within our society. I wish to promote a universal American dream for all within our borders and abroad. Almost everything that is written within these pages has been done so through my strict and sincere dedication to educating myself throughout the entirety of my life, even when having endured physical and mental hardships in the past. It was not intellectuals who gave me the courage to write this work, no, but instead the four classes of people that I have encountered in my life. Those being the farmer, the worker, the soldier, and the scholar. In recent times, mainly within the past 44 years, we have gradually submitted and given our country to gangsters and prostitutes by making them idol celebrities, permitting the moral decadence of our society.

One of the things that is an issue with this country is that the older generation shoots down the ideas of the younger generation, never allowing them to think outside of their stubborn box. There is a thing called handing down the torch to people who are more younger and innovative. Yet there is also a thing called remembering your ancestors and honoring in them in memory as well as through human action in the realm of both communal and private initiative.

Perhaps most will be unwilling to forgive me for writing this piece, but I say let them think as they will for that is their own individual free born right guaranteed to them by Mother Nature herself once you're excreted from the womb to the day of your inevitable demise. The people at large can do what they want with this work, but I do not advocate, nor wish to ever advocate, anything that'd be devastating to the US, the land of my fathers for four generations, as a whole. It's all very baffling to the untrained eye to interpret and comprehend, yet take a step back and you'll see how much of an art of ideological war and grandly beautiful picture it is. As Sun Tzu said, "Sometimes the best way to win a war is by not fighting at all."

ECONOMICAL ETHICS

People need to look into things by studying or analyzing their environment to draw conclusions of their own. Every person has that ability and right, and it should not be imposed on someone just because you disagree with them. They should try and find a common ground in which they'll potentially comprehend each other as well as make a compromise that'll appeal to both parties involved. Don't get these ideals wrong though, sometimes primitive force is the only means, but that depends on how radically fanatical that person is within their beliefs to where they indulge in terrorist activities and trample the free born civil rights granted by both nature and the will of the people.

If you ask me, what this country needs is an alternate party from the Democrats & Republicans. It needs something new, something fresh to encourage the hearts, will, and tenacious mind of the people. A new party, one that respects the rights of the individual, should come into the field of American politics. One that encourages academic intellectual and physical labor for people of all races, colors, ethnicities, sexes, and religions. The religious part should be studied merely from a skeptical theological point of view. The Independent Party is a good choice.

I admit that with my own character and principles, I try and strive to be socialist in heart and capitalist in mind. Whenever I fall short of a goal, I internally berate myself to drive myself towards perfection. A person and worker's true value as an individual is not, nor should not, be dictated by the height of their wages but by their own strict devotional work ethic and drive to see things through both inside the work place and at home in physical and intellectual labor.

People, regardless of wealth or status, should go on about thoroughly studying economics from Keynesianomics, the Austrian School of Economics, socialism, capitalism, and communism. From my perspective socialism should not be imposed upon the people by the government they put into power, but be practiced in a philanthropic and philosophical way with the people happily giving a portion of what they can of the wealth they've attained in their own doing so, rather than through heavy taxation.

We must split the socialist and capitalist economic principles in people's own character because a person must be tactical. But not only that, a person should, yes, drive themselves to accumulate wealth and distribute a portion of it to society as a whole. As it says in the Bible, "Love thy neighbor." What better way to love a neighbor than providing financial support to help see them through their own hardships and goals? We must retain the socialist ideology in heart through our own private yearning to do good for others.

Socialism, despite being widely imposed upon various states in the world, unfortunately doesn't work in actual practice when it's forced upon a population. It's good and intriguing in theory and on paper, but doesn't work on an economic level. It should only be, in my opinion, an academic philosophy that a person dedicates themselves to. Seizing the means of production sounds good to Marxists, who exercise socialism to the extreme with having the state control over various sectors of human society, but we already have that with working in the various fields that we choose and encouraging communal goodness.

If it's used in its purest form, such as with the Soviet Union and all their former allies, it doesn't entirely work, especially with sanctions imposed upon them. In fact the Soviet Union under Joseph Stalin brought in capitalistic western industrialists, scientists, and engineers to help push the country forward with Stalin's dream of perfecting their workers' paradise. Leon Trotsky, one of Stalin's rivals within the Bolshevik Party, wanted to continue the communist revolution by expanding it to other nations throughout the globe before they so called "perfected" it at home in their nation of the former Russian Empire. For many people Karl Marx's work "The Communist Manifesto" has some good points here and there, which it does, but it is mostly unsettling, asinine, and disturbing for the taste of society as a whole to practice in an economic way. It's good in theory and on paper, but in actual practice doesn't work. Even more so with politicians making numerous promises of free services and institutions funded by the whole state. That's all done though to promote their constituent power base, the mass mob of ignorant oafs, who'd gladly toss someone into the spotlight for a mere 30 pieces of silver.

Keynesian economics, which is technically rudimentary socialism, was intended by the economic theorist John Maynard Keynes to be used temporarily in the event of economic crisis with shifting high taxes to various corporations & business and allow small businesses to thrive with lowering their taxes. Then when the economy either started to become or came to the right point it was stable those high taxes would be shifted to the small businesses that were allowed to prosper during the recession. Those accumulated taxes would then be invested in various public social programs and projects to promote employment during the recession and then those services could be shifted towards private interests once the economy stabilized. It has been said even that Hitler and his National Socialist German Workers' Party discovered Keynesianomics before John M. Keynes came out with his economic theoretical work "The General Theory of Employment, Interest, and Money" in 1935. Now, both that form of economic theory & practice as well as the Austrian School of Economics (capitalism) are great areas of study that people must be willing to take into consideration and study. If people wish to study more into the economics that bridge the gap between socialism, capitalism, and democracy then I suggest reading the book "Capitalism, Socialism, and Democracy" by Joseph A. Schumpeter.

People like to think that because you have a booming economy that means you have a decreasing national deficit. No, that's a huge misconception. The two are not the same. They are separate. Take a look into Nazi Germany with the Reichsbank and the MEFO Bills brought into being by economic thinker and banker Hjalmar Schacht for instance. That, or the Reagan years and Trump years.

The MEFO Bills distributed by a bank that the Nazis controlled were interest free forms of credit that were used by industrialists within Nazi Germany to promote their businesses as well as fuel the German war machine before the outbreak of WWII. It was a way for the government to cover up expenses that were made to promote the production of military armaments and vehicles. When the time came for those bills to be repaid, the Nazis distributed out bonds, printed money with no backing except through the concept of Fiat money, as well as took away the savings of various citizens to help pay for some of the debt. All that piled on top of the already existing previous debt of the Weimar Republic. That is one of the reasons to why they started WWII because they needed to conquer territory and abscond with the riches from those territories to cover their financial losses and debt.

Now, with Reagan and his Trickle-Down Theory it did promote the US economy in the 80's. However, he promoted military spending both openly and covertly with the Iran-Contra Affair from 1985-1987 and funding the Mujihadeen in Afghanistan during the Soviet-Afghan War from 1979-1989. The US national debt though rose from just under 1 trillion dollars to 3 trillion dollars over the course of his two terms. The succeeding President, George HW Bush, continued much of his policies and brought the debt to 4 trillion dollars.

With Trump's version of Trickle-Down Economics, he, without a doubt, greatly promoted the US economy during his term, except during his last year due to Covid-19 breaking out globally from China. The debt rose though from 19.8 trillion dollars to over 27 trillion dollars, and that was just his first term.

INTEREST, LOAN & CENTRAL BANKING

With interest rates, loans, and value of the US dollar that is mainly determined by the Federal Reserve Bank of the US, which functions as our central bank. It is in place to promote and regulate the economy with keeping the US dollar at a stable point and not have it go through rapid hyperinflation in the event of major economic crises. That, as well as exchange our money with help from the IRS to various businesses within the US and abroad that could be hit heavily by an economic depression and recession. They raise interest rates to not only limit and at times discourage the amount of loans distributed but to have a higher revenue yield to supply their coffers. It follows and is the principle and practice of usury. It can be beneficial to have, especially in times of war or even some economic crises when security bonds, also known as bearer bonds, are distributed to the populace in limited numbers through various private and public companies as well as services. Those bonds are subject to compound interest and inflation, meaning their value will greatly increase over time. However, the downside to bonds is that they are unregistered and therefore untraceable. So, the actual owner of a bearer bond is determined by who physically holds the paper in their hands.

With the Federal Reserve being a centralized bank, it was brought into existence by the US government under President Woodrow Wilson. Now, the Federal Reserve is its own agency and entity that is not under the strict control of the government yet works in tandem with it to help regulate and keep our economy stable.

In regard to economic crises, such as depressions and recessions, they normally handout money with the permission of Congress and the IRS to various crucially large and small businesses. They mainly focus on large businesses though since they employ the most people and are crucial to maintaining the economic standing of the country. Recently though they have distributed bailout money through economic care packages approved by Congress to the everyday US citizen and worker to prevent them from going hungry, promote consumerism for a time, and to help pay their bills. The second of means of financial action in times of economic action with distributing those care packages to everyday citizens is the best alternative.

EDUCATION

Another thing this country needs is hard driven workers with a common goal and competent politicians both young and old, but with term restrictions, to help lead them into a brighter future for the American dream.

Our government and mixed market economy is in need of reminding the individual citizen, each and everyone of us, that competition drives innovation. Too much over bearing bureaucratic red tape and regulation of large businesses is more of a hinderance to the very productivity of society. Collectivization can be beneficial and effective, but that's if it is used sparingly and in consideration of the staff and tools at the disposal of all kinds of businesses as well as public services. Yes, regulation of free market competition should be used, yet even that itself should be sparingly so as to not step on the rights of those businesses as well as to encourage amiable cooperation between those businesses and government officials.

Education is a crucial thing within a society. It must be provided by both the state and through privatized institutions and communities. It should encourage ideological intellectual contemplation, develop social skills that are good in centralizing a common goal of maintaining discipline and order, as well as physical prowess with allowing their students to practice almost any sport that they wish. We're still animals, primates within the eyes and laws of nature. We are not above nature for we, collectively as a species, developed through years of environmental and ideological evolution. Evolution does not just stop. That is asinine and goes against everything the laws of nature stand for as well as the grand scheme of the Almighty Creator. He gives us power not only in physical being but also ideologically. We are made in his image not in the physical sense because to do so would require either a strong gene pool to do so or a cloning machine. We are made in his image through the ideological and philosophical sense and way. Individuality must be cherished. No one individual is above the group, yet the group as a whole must respect the rights of the individual.

Now, to get back on track with education. The educational system in America is appallingly shattered and broken. We have the various educational institutions within this grand democratic nation of ours to fully implement drilling students within the halls of academic and vocational principle and teachings towards a better tomorrow for all the communities. However, vocational trade schools have distanced themselves from those who have the strict physical determination, will, and merit to do so. They now mainly focus on academic achievement with those who have high grades and aren't regularly sick, absent from class. They are more of a fraternity now if out of anything. In the past they were not always like this, they allowed either individual boys or girls or both together collectively to attend their institutions. They have strict qualifications for students to join merely for the sake of encouraging the state of pumping more money into them, yet they shoot the whole of the community around them in the foot by doing so. It is selective favoritism at its grandest and unjust podium. There is a demographic and they should not marginalize those who work their asses off to pursue trades, yet aren't good academically. Vocational schools are a great asset to have if a person wishes to quickly and initially join the vocational workforce outside of school right after graduation.

With academic schools, they are a fine thing that develops social skills for students, provide a sense of fun, and learning for the youth. They help them build and renew memory with having them be taught the various sciences, history, politics, languages, and even; although I don't fully agree with it since church and state should be separate to avoid a theocratic state; religions from across the globe. However, even they have submitted to greed and wish to not have certain students learn vocational trades because it'll take away the funding from them if they go away and transfer to another school.

Universities and colleges are fine, and further drive a person towards perfection within their field or fields of study. However, they're overwhelmingly expensive, even when you have grants from both profit or nonprofit organizations. They're even very expensive with scholarships from the schools they attended. The tragic thing is public schools and parents nowadays force college onto children, making them feel they will not have success and be a contributor to society if they don't attend and learn there. Do you really think every 17-23 year old or older person knows exactly what they want to study? No, you don't. Hell, even they don't fully know themselves. Many go in thinking they know what they want for a major, grow tired and lose interest in it, choose not to pursue it after graduation, or can't find a job in it.

The bottom line is with education as a whole is that all our institutions should be working in tandem as brothers in arms for the good of the whole national and global community. They should not be squabbling and pulling the children, the youth of which carries the legacy of our ancestors. What our ancestors and forefathers as well as foremothers achieved was not handed and given to them. No, they created it themselves through blood, toil, tears, and sweat to provide for themselves and everyone around them.

HEALTHCARE SYSTEM

When it comes to healthcare, I personally feel it should be a state's choice to choose whether or not they want it privatized or subsidized. Having subsidized healthcare much like the Canadian model is a lovely and indeed thoughtful idea, however, we cannot as a sophisticatedly developed mixed market economy fully allow our healthcare to be placed under strict state control. That, as well as impose a state of dependency upon the whole US population from Hawaii & Alaska to New York & Maine as well as from New Mexico & Texas to North Dakota & Minnesota. The reason for that is even state run programs can be inefficient and require too much red tape for a medical patient to receive basic care, even for something as minor as an accidental razor cut to the neck from when you shave. There's also the fact certain individuals maybe wrong for the job, especially within the realm of psychiatric care. All the fancy little diplomas they, some psychiatrists or physical medical doctors, usually have plastered on their office walls is just a cry of attention and making themselves look to be perfectly qualified to handle a person's issues on the outside as a presentation of their so called "qualifications". Yet inside, they're just overly stubborn, judgmental, inconsiderate, legal medical drug pushing, incompetent, pompous shits who dread their profession and just want to get through the day without thoroughly considering other prognosis on the well-being of their patients. Some won't even listen if you tell them of the negative side effects you have experienced from their treatment, which includes the medication they put you on. They'll just have you continue it or push you onto something worse. Then there are some doctors who make it a strict routine to drug test their patients for each appointment so they can make more money off your insurance. Now, imagine you as a tax payer having to pay for that with universal healthcare, which is funded by you and the various businesses throughout the US. Despite those points, there is a bright side to universal healthcare, the various companies and public services that operate under it do not have the unjust, arbitrary, and inconsiderate policies of a fully privatized healthcare system that treats people more like sickly cattle. Some fully privatized healthcare companies deny service to clients who have pre-existing conditions, like having a minor or severe birth defect, beyond their control. Healthcare is a sensitive and crucial part of society, one in which we cannot do without. Still, it should be decided individually from state to state from south to north and east to west in the US if they wish to have either a fully privatized or subsidized healthcare system in place.

Then there is the thought of having the Internal Revenue Service and Department of Justice cracking down on multimillion to multi-trillion dollar companies, their CEOs and executive boards down to the lowest level supervisor to attempt to generate revenue for the US by preventing them from pushing their money to foreign banks. Almost everyone knows this as the Panama Papers. This is also an idea that holds a degree of merit because most companies do do that to evade the IRS's collections and the high taxes of our country. However, it would be too much for both departments to handle alone and even collectively within a centralized committee of agency representative officials to manage if it were done on all of them simultaneously. Those various agency officials would have to be working round the clock to find any kind of discrepancies, go through the court systems to bring those companies and individuals before a state hearing, gather witnesses and physical paper as well as computerized digital proof from social media platforms as well as from the overall internet cloud system. They'd have to even dive into the dark web, perhaps even have people go undercover in a sense to gather all the info necessary to win their cases against the army of lawyers they have at their disposal. That, and there is the fact that that committee may even be bought out by a certain company to take another of their rivals down for them. It would be almost completely wholesale moral and financial corruption run amuck. It should be done tactically and slowly, not all at once. Even then, yes it is supposedly illegal for companies and their executives to push their earnings and savings to foreign nations outside the US, but our government and the basic ideals of a mixed market economy and of our Founding Fathers permit them to do so. Companies still put their profits and shares into foreign banks not just to avoid the IRS and heavy taxation but because they have businesses across the globe. They need that portion of their revenue on standby in those foreign nations to help fund their business and financial interests within those countries at a moment's notice, instead of having to wire directly to the US based headquarters to gather the finances they require to fuel their endeavors and interests. There is also the fact that both the DOJ and IRS have to deal with not just businesses and their executives but with the everyday American citizen and proletariat for numerous things from the plain minor trivial or crucially large reasons of which are extensive and won't be mentioned in this work. It also breaks into the realm of a violation of privacy, which every individual, which includes corporations, are privileged to have. That is not just within the confines of nature itself without our sophistication but also within the confines of the artificial administrative and societal constructs we have in place to protect the unalienable individual rights of everyone. New laws would either have to be rapidly written plus put into place if it is all done at a rushed tone at once, or put together gradually with permitting such a collective investigative revenue committee to do those things one business at a time. It comes down to a simple consideration of math in regards to physical man power, time, how many businesses they're tackling, and overall energy alongside strict devotion of a person to see such a feat through.

INTEREST & USURY

In the realms of interest and loans, especially through the distribution of bonds, it is crucial to have a centralized bank to regulate the flow and value of a nation's or multiple nations' currencies to prevent them from faltering and becoming in a sense worthless through hyperinflation.

POLITICAL CRITICISMS

CRITICISMS OF TRUMP

When Trump was in power, I disagreed with his policy
and promise of building a wall along the US-Mexico border.
That's a huge 1948-1954 mile long border. The wall would
have to cross through mountains, rugged terrain, deserts,
rivers and streams, and through both public/private
properties. It'd take more than the projected $20 billion he
thought it would to make since he'd have to pay engineers,
construction crews, unions, forward construction
observers, and the overall material it would take to build it.
It'd cost more to keep it maintained in the long run. Not
only that, you'd have to have a reinforced border patrol
along there to frequently inspect the wall as well as make
sure immigrants haven't tunneled underneath it. The
Mexican Cartel could easily do that like the Vietcong did in
French-Indo China from the 1950's-1975 against both the
French and American forces there. It would also disturb a
vast ecosystem, making it more harmful to the
environment. Then there was that spy drone debacle with

China during the first couple months of his Presidency where he initially said that China should just keep it. That was completely asinine because China, despite producing goods for the US, is an economic as well as military rival not only within the Asian continent, but the whole world. I couldn't help but think that the Chinese may reverse engineer our drone to gain further understanding of our technology so they could potentially use it against us.

Also, during almost all three of Trump's presidential election campaigns he has accepted endorsements from Neo-Nazi groups such as the KKK and perhaps even the Aryan Union. He's also, without a doubt, received endorsements from various businesses and powers outside the US. These types of individual groups are ones of which should not have any significant say within our current as well as future administrative system, especially the racial segregationist and persecutive groups. Any candidate who accepts those types of endorsements has not only degraded their own moral, rational, and considerate standing but sold themselves as well as their constituents within society as a whole out for a mere thirty pieces of silver. America is, yes, the home of the free and the brave in which freedom of speech and the press is crucial to maintain a sense of self assurance that our rights, guaranteed by the US constitution, will never be trampled. However, when a group of people are marginalized through brutish and ideological methods it is unjust and should not be encouraged as well as praised. This especially applies to foreigners who came here through the morally and legally right way through hard work and dedication to learn the American way of life. We are, all of us, in this together to see the American way of life preserved. The American dream and way of life should not require us to be harshly divided into just individual groups of wealth, ethnicities, sexual attractions, nationalities, race, skin color, religious ideologies, and stubborn political backgrounds.

In regard to the Aryan Union perhaps backing Donald Trump, they are many of themselves ignorant and deceived. They buy into the narrative that the white man, especially those of Nordic descent, are the master race. They do not even know what a true Aryan is. An Aryan is not a gloriously tall, strong, intelligent, and powerful blonde haired and blue eyed child and person at all. If you want to know what a true Aryan is, then look towards the Middle East and southwestern parts of Asia, most notably India. The Aryans were Indo-Iranians; who were merchants, soldiers, and traders; that constantly migrated from Iran & Iraq to various parts of southwestern Asia roughly around 3,800 years ago. They're mentioned in the Hindu Mahabharata and various Vedas. The term Aryan was unfortunately in 19th century Europe changed and used by various racially motivated groups, who wanted to thrust any foreigners out from their native soil to keep their communities pure to their eyes. Adolf Hitler and the National Socialist German Workers' Party took this concept and ideology to the extreme and wished to use it as a socio-political means to promote their constituent base as well as to foment the false narrative ideal that the German and, therefore, the whole Nordic community have a deeper and more significant role within the course of not just the past but the ultimate future of humanity.

There is no master race. We as a human species, yes, are divided into races. We have whites, blacks, latinos, orientals, and Native Americans. However, we exist together on this planet, breath the same air, and bleed the same blood regardless of nationality, religion, wealth status, sex, the two natural genders, ethnicity, and overall creed. To move forward as a species such divisions must be ideologically torn down to permit us to walk together as brothers and sisters towards a new heaven, a new Garden of Eden. Yet we cannot fully forget the past. The dead that came before us must be honored in memory.

CRITICISMS OF BIDEN

In the regards to the Keystone Pipeline the decision Biden made on it should be reversed. It would be economically beneficial, it would reduce the US's dependency on foreign oil shipments and reserves, greatly reduce the labor for it for other countries and ours, but the labor that'd be cut in our country could be diverted to the pipeline construction. It would also be environmentally sound, appealing to environmentalists; despite what the Democrats say; since it'd reduce the gas and oil CO_2 emissions from all the ships coming to the US and possibly close regions abroad. That reduction of CO_2 emissions and other gases will be better for the atmosphere and possibly help reduce global warming in the grand scheme of things. Hypothetically speaking, if there ever were to be found oil in another South American country, we Americans could link the pipelines up across the whole Northern & Southern American continents.

Those US economic and political actions could possibly strengthen the US dollar, lessen our dependence on Saudi Arabia's oil and various other countries in the mid-east. That Saudi oil as well as Kuwait, Iraq, Iran, and other Middle Eastern states could then have their collective resources be diverted to African countries if they, the African continent as a whole much like the US & Europe, had a strong central currency to trade with the Middle Eastern countries. However, it is almost impossible to do so due to various treaties and political agreements made outside of official government overseeing of which enforce them, but don't officially recognize. Case in point the Sykes-Picot Agreement made by the British Empire and the French Republic through British civil servant Mark Sykes and French civil servant Francois G. Picot to thoroughly divide the Ottoman Empire; they were a central power allied nation to the German Empire and Austrian-Hungarian Empire; at the end of WWI into respective protectorate states. However, Sykes later on wanted to somewhat do away with that agreement to allow the Arab Revolt, which was supplied and aided mainly by the British Empire with their field officer T.E. Lawrence (aka Lawrence of Arabia) to unite all the Arab tribes and communities throughout the Middle East into a single nation. That idea was shot down though because of varying religious and imperialist reasons that shall not be mentioned in this work. If people wish to learn more, then they should read "Lawrence in Arabia" by Scott Anderson as well as see the near four hour long movie Lawrence of Arabia.

As for Biden and the Democratic Party's determined endeavor to impose strict gun laws, there is some sense of them. They're trying to reduce the number of mass shootings by requiring those who purchase, sell weapons, and/or apply for the licenses to carry to undergo psychological evaluation and to prohibit certain weapons and their accessories from being sold to the general populace. However, similar efforts were made in the past by previous nations such as Nazi Germany in regards to the Nuremberg Laws that restricted many of the natural rights for the peoples they considered to be inferior and leeching parasites on the German nation They marginalized that community not just through prohibiting them from owning businesses and providing for themselves. They also stripped them of the means to effectively defend themselves in the event that they're systematically and brutally persecuted as well as exterminated. Various communist countries impose such restrictions and regulations upon their own populace still to this day. Such a thing, even in a democratic institution and society, must never be fully practiced for the people as a whole. The military industrial complex and law enforcement officials mustn't be the only ones permitted to carry firearms since they could easily impose any harsh law upon us that greatly violates our own individual unalienable rights from freedom of speech and expression to life, liberty, property, and the pursuit of happiness. The British even did so both before and during the American Revolutionary War with attempting and even succeeding here & there with taking away the colonists' weapons used for defense and hunting to put food on their table. The idea of universal restrictions on guns is, in my own opinion, absurd and asinine. That is because people would be willing to toss away one of their most crucial rights, apart from freedom of speech & expression, for a sense of security that is rather false. Various Cartels and Mafias could easily smuggle guns into our country through the borders and overseas cargo shipments and make potentially millions on the black market as people are being systematically extorted and robbed in their very own neighborhoods.

US-RUSSIAN RELATIONS

One of the issues with US-Russian relations is that there is still a lingering sentiment and policy of Cold War pseudo-imperialistic dogma in the endeavor of containment of communism. One in which they're not directly fighting against each other, but using proxy states and puppets to do so for them. There was and to a degree still is an ideological and economic war between NATO and the Soviet's Warsaw Pact. The Warsaw Pact was created after NATO to attempt to combat it as well as to spread the ideals of varying teachings of Marxism, mainly Marxist-Leninism and Marxist-Stalinism. Marxist-Trotskyism was too revolutionary, outwardly aggressive, and did not focus on the problems at home. Such an example is clearly pointed at within the pages of the political allegory "Animal Farm" by George Orwell.

The western capitalist countries though have themselves to blame though for fueling the Russian Revolution covertly by providing funding through various avenues of

Wall Street. Stalin took advantage of such ties to bring in western industrialists, scientists, and engineers to help push the Soviet economy forward in the 1920's-40's until the start of the Cold War when both they and the Western Allies pulled in Nazi scientists and officials, many of whom were pardoned of war crimes and crimes against humanity, to gain an advantage over the other. The rest is history.

Now, onto the Russian-Ukraine War. That is a war being waged by the Russians and Ukrainians with their NATO allies, mainly the US, aiding them by providing money and weapons to fend off their Russo and Slavic brothers and sisters. Ukraine does, yes, want to join NATO, but that goes against previously signed treaties and agreements made between the former Soviet Union and the western half of Europe as well as the US that states that former Soviet satellite countries are pretty much fully prohibited to join NATO. The people of both countries don't want that war. No, instead it is the politicians and military officials they have put into power. In my honest opinion, those regions of which Russia has control over and wish collectively as a people to be Russian should be permitted to secede from Ukraine and be absolved into the Russian Federation under Vladimir Putin, whilst allowing the other remaining portion of Ukraine to join NATO or at least be kicked out of it in honor of the previously agreed upon treaties and policies.

US-CHINESE RELATIONS

When it comes to US-Chinese relations that is a sensitive and hard topic, but yet a fairly rational and ethical thing to understand. Don't get me wrong, it is crucial that we still as not only a nation but as a world through the European Union and United Nations monitor and keep an eye on communists. To dive fully wholesale into socialistic and communistic economic principles can lead to the degradation and ruin of a society. Take a look at Cambodia for instance in the 1960's-70's.

Both China and the U.S. have each other by the balls though since China is basically a huge manufacturing country of which we have taken advantage of through their communistic government. Many of our manufacturing companies within the US have outsourced their work to them due to the cheap labor since our currency is stronger than theirs. If hostilities were to ever rise between the US and China as well as their communistic allies, the US could pull those varying companies interests out of there, greatly weakening their economy. You can thank Richard Nixon for opening up China to the US during the Vietnam War to promote US relations in Asia, as well as to promote his own constituent base with not just voters but businesses, too. When it comes down to it though, it wasn't just Nixon who sold out our economic advantage but also Chinese Communist Party leader Mao Zedong with straying away from Marxist ideology in the economic sense with having capitalist interests come into their country to help build it. They, the Chinese Communist Party, needed our aid since they could not heavily rely on the Soviets, North Koreans, Cuba, and the various states of the former French-Indo China territory that belonged to the French Republic as a protectorate colony & state.